The Stillness We Seek

Daily Meditations for Advent

Cathy H. George

FORWARD MOVEMENT
Cincinnati, Ohio

Reprinted 2015
© 2011 Forward Movement

Forward Movement
412 Sycamore Street
Cincinnati, Ohio 45202-4194

800.543.1813
www.forwardmovement.org

Library of Congress Cataloging-in-Publication Data
George, Cathy H.
 The stillness we seek : daily meditations for Advent / Cathy H.
George. —
1st ed.
    p. cm.
 ISBN 978-0-88028-327-4
1. Advent—Meditations. I. Title. II. Title: Daily meditations for
Advent.
 BV40.G46 2011
 242'.332—dc23
                                        2011022917
Printed in the United States of America

Scripture quotations are from the New Revised Standard
Version Bible, © 1989 by National Council of the Churches of
Christ in the United States of America. Used by permission.
All rights reserved.

Psalm passages are from the Psalter in *The Book of Common Prayer*.

Page 84: Thurman, Howard. "The Work of Christmas," from
A Mood of Christmas and Other Celebrations. Friends United Press
(www.fum.org/shop): Richmond, IN, 1985, reprinted 2011.
Used with permission.

The Stillness We Seek

Preface

"Cast away the works of darkness, and put on the armor of light." So says the collect for the First Sunday of Advent in *The Book of Common Prayer.*

Perhaps more than any other time of year, these four weeks preceding Christmas Day and the twelve days after are a time when the church invites us to come in from what goes on outside. Through the prayers, readings, colors, and silence of our worship, we are given the spiritual refreshment and guidance we seek. The colors of Advent are stunning and rich: royal blue, purple, rose, and white. The stillness we seek in the midst of all the activity around us is found in the centering power of the Savior whose birth we await.

Advent is filled with expectation and sometimes disappointment. The days before Christmas are sacred. We want to make time for prayer. We look forward to annual concerts and pageants, as well as seeing and hearing from people we care about. In the midst of our hopes for the season we also encounter traffic jams, ornery people, lists with more to be done than we have time for, and long lines in stores. We miss people we love who have died; we may grieve a divorce or feel the loneliness of being single. Maybe we are angry over losing a job. Advent is a time of year when we often experience conflict between our hopes for peace and joy and the commercial and social demands made upon us.

The secret to living fully might be simply to *be* where we are, keenly aware of the present moment. In the next four weeks we will pause to pray and seek the peace that is always there in the midst of whatever else we are doing. We will sing: "Come, thou long expected Jesus, born to set thy people free; from our fears and sins release us, let us find our rest in thee" (*The Hymnal 1982*, #66). I pray that those words will come true for you this Advent.

A woman I admire lost her husband in a helicopter crash when their four children were very young. She never missed church on Sunday but rarely spoke of her faith. I wondered whether her faith helped her at the time of this tragic loss, and when I asked her she replied, "Sometimes all you can do is read the psalms." These meditations are dedicated to her. They are inspired by a line from a psalm appointed for each day in Advent through Epiphany from the Daily Office lectionary in *The Book of Common Prayer*.

Cathy H. George
Dorchester, Massachusetts

First Sunday of Advent

But the LORD has pleasure in those who fear him,
in those who await his gracious favor.

—Psalm 147:12

Take your time. So often we are in a hurry, rushing between one thing and the next. We usually try to use our time efficiently and effectively. Advent begins with the reminder to wait upon God. So as we begin, we give to God the simple gift of our time.

Remember Fred Rogers in the children's program *Mr. Rogers' Neighborhood?* He took his time. He did one thing at a time, and did it fully, whether it was changing from his outdoor jacket and hanging it in the closet to change into his indoor sweater, or sitting down to change from his dress shoes to his sneakers. He took his time and was present to what he was doing. Children were drawn to his calm. Mr. Rogers gave you his full and complete attention.

As you pray, give it your full attention. Take your time. What we seek in prayer is not a state of peace or bliss. We don't pray in order to "get something out of it." Our success at prayer will not be anything particular that happens while we pray; it is simply doing it each day and not giving up. It does not matter if your mind wanders to mundane details. Gently, firmly, repeatedly invite it back.

We do not pray in order to accomplish something; we pray to increase the space in our life for God. Today I pray for the grace to do one thing at a time, and to do it with my complete and full attention.

One of the most important things in our prayer
is the eagerness and confidence with which
we throw ourselves open to his perpetual coming.
There should always be more waiting
than striving in a Christian prayer.

—Evelyn Underhill
Christian mysticist
(1875-1941)

First Monday of Advent

Submit to the LORD with fear,
and with trembling bow before him.

—Psalm 2:11

When my daughter was a toddler, she awoke from her nap in the early dusk of late December afternoons. She climbed into her stroller and I pushed it over the bumpy neighborhood sidewalk in the fresh, cold air in the last light before supper. As darkness descended, candles were lit, lights came on, and smells of supper cooking were in the air.

We passed reindeer on roofs, Santas in sleighs, colored lights marking the edges of homes, and candy canes bordering sidewalks. She pointed and screamed with delight, but it was only when she reached the plastic nativity scene, lit from within, that she began twisting in her stroller and pulling at the straps across her tummy to get out and touch it. Pulling off her blue mittens, she walked to Mary and touched her red plastic lips. She knelt down to see baby Jesus, glued to the manger.

"What does the cow say?" I asked.

"Moo," she said, "and the sheep say 'Baaa!'"

I lured her away from the figures by offering her a lollipop from my pocket if she climbed back into the stroller. She leaned to one side to look back until the nativity scene was out of sight.

In Montreal's old city, a larger-than-life nativity scene is crawling with children. A little boy pushes his foot against Mary's head scarf as he climbs onto the back of a cow. Two girls hold the hands of the magi, making their threesome a group of five. Other children hold the ears of the donkey like reins on a horse.

God comes to us in a story we know, with animals, a mom, a dad, a baby, and a place to "lay down his sweet head." The sparkling eyes of children at play display the power of the story of God incarnate. Divine love comes down and stoops to our humanity. God is never the same again, and we are never the same again. In the middle of holiday shopping, in the center of the city, we meet the story of God taking on human form. We behold the glory that shines in the darkness, and the darkness cannot overcome it (John 1:5). We touch the majesty of God with the smallest of fingers and everything in us is well, anointed by Jesus' coming to be with us.

First Tuesday of Advent

*In the morning, LORD, you hear my voice;
early in the morning I make my appeal
and watch for you.*

—Psalm 5:3

Six of us gathered in the pews on Wednesday night for Bible study. A tall, thin man from Jamaica came early to turn on the heat and lights, and he opened our meeting with prayer. He gave thanks for God's protection in getting us all safely to the church. At the close of our discussion, a woman from Trinidad who wore a stylish leopard-skin hat closed our discussion with prayers for safety and protection on our way home and throughout the coming week. Then out we ventured into the darkness.

Where I live, Advent arrives to a world gone gray—the muted earth; the slate blue winter sky; barren, black trees against the horizon at dusk. It is dark in the morning and dark again by late afternoon. We put on the season of Advent like armor as we step into the regular practice of prayer this month before Christmas, an armor of light against the darkness.

Darkness comes in the Advent season in many forms. The darkness of violence in the inner city, the darkness of loss in the midst of a joyous season, the darkness of the voice that seeks to draw us away from God, insistent and intelligent.

Maybe you did not find time to read your Advent meditation and pray yesterday, failing already so early in the season to live up to your Advent commitment. The power of darkness will take hold of the smallest blip, the tiniest mistake, and blow it up, to make of it as much of a roadblock to God as we will allow.

Yesterday is behind you. Begin fresh today; make your appeal, as the psalm says. God hearkens to a cry for help.

Almighty God, give us grace to cast away
the works of darkness, and put on the armor of light,
now in the time of this mortal life.

Collect for the First Sunday of Advent,
—*The Book of Common Prayer*

First Wednesday of Advent

How long, O LORD?
Will you forget me for ever?
How long will you hide your face from me?
How long shall I have perplexity in my mind,
and grief in my heart, day after day?

—Psalm 13:1-2

Cleaning house in exchange for my rent and securing a loan to cover my tuition, I enrolled in seminary. My final year, while making my way through the ordination process, I was also going through a divorce. I met with my bishop and he told me that he wanted me to step out of the ordination process. I felt forgotten by God. All I heard the bishop say was "no," when what he said was "not now."

I had "perplexity in my mind, and grief in my heart, day after day," as the psalmist says. I awoke to a dream in which I was the only person left on a subway train, cut off by constantly closing doors and unable to find my way in the gray underground maze. I was angry with God.

When a friend who teaches a course on prayer lost her newborn child at birth, she stopped praying. She felt God had hidden from her and abandoned her. One day she was seized by anger and began pounding a pillow and yelling. It was then that she sensed the presence of God. Her fists were beating on the sacred heart of Jesus. He came to her in her anger, when she could not go to him.

Anger does not evaporate into thin air as we might hope. Anger is energy that arises for a reason, often to protect us or alert us. When we ignore it, it festers.

Is it okay to be angry with God? Yes, we get angry with those we love. The psalms give us the words we may not be able to find on our own to express our anger at God. Anger can be holy; God wants to be with us in everything we experience. In all things, in all moods, at all times. When you cannot find God, when you have shut God out in your anger, ask God to find you.

Look upon me and answer me, O LORD my God.

—Psalm 13:3

Advent and Christmas Meditations

First Thursday of Advent

He brought me out into an open place;
he rescued me because he delighted in me.

—Psalm 18:20

I grew up on a farm in the Midwest. Open spaces were a constant part of the landscape of my childhood. The field behind the barn led to twenty acres of open meadow where my dad mowed trails for walking and skiing.

In high school, when the cool kids invited me to their parties, I filled my cup with beer like everyone else and held it up to my mouth as if drinking it. When no one was looking, I poured it out on the bushes so I could refill it and appear to be fitting in. I was desperate to be liked and was willing to play along to be included. It felt lonely to be with people while pretending to be someone I wasn't. One night I got a ride home after a party that followed a football game. Confused and sad, instead of going into the house, I walked "out into an open place." The air was clear and I lay on my back on a knoll in the meadow and looked up at the night sky filled with stars. God "rescued me because he delighted in me." God broke into the lonely world of a teenaged girl trying to fit in by bringing her out to an open place.

Outside of God everything is narrow. God is not a restrictive presence. God does not box us in. God brings us out to an open place, a place where we are reawakened to who we are. God does not nail us down, cramp us up, or confine us—God sets us free.

Find your way to an open place today, in the country or in the city, by the side of a river, the balcony of your building, the playing field where you run, the golf course, the park, a meadow. When you arrive, pray to God who delights in you and brings you out to an open place.

The walls I build are not your boundaries.
Lord, lead me to an open place.
Amen.

First Friday of Advent

Keep me as the apple of your eye;
hide me under the shadow of your wings.

—Psalm 17:8

In fifth grade I began taking flute lessons, much to my grandfather's delight. He gave me a box of chocolates to show his support of me. On the inside cover of the box, a small circle matching the placement of each chocolate identified that piece's ingredients: milk chocolate with caramel, dark chocolate with almonds. It was the first box of chocolates I was ever given. I read every word on the inside cover, over and over and over. I was the apple of my grandfather's eye.

In the majesty of divine love, each of us is the apple of God's eye. We do not share the attention of God. I don't know how it works, but God does. Each of us is God's only child, and God does not ration time, decide who is most in need or most deserving, listen to who screams the loudest, or look for the tallest in the crowd. God's ways are not our ways. We have God's complete and full attention, all the time, even when we don't want it.

One of the methods used by the power of evil is to place us in competition with each other. The devil wants us to think God's mercy is limited and we are being a nuisance to take God's time with our petty worries when the people of Haiti and in so many other parts of the world are tragically suffering. Don't listen to that voice. It is not telling the truth.

When you turn to God today to pray, remember you are the apple of God's eye. You have God's attention as if you were the only person in the world. Just as the people of Haiti do.

For you yourself created my inmost parts;
you knit me together in my mother's womb.
I will thank you because I am marvelously made;
your works are wonderful, and I know it well.

—Psalm 139:12-13

First Saturday of Advent

Some put their trust in chariots
and some in horses,
but we will call upon
the Name of the LORD our God.
They collapse and fall down,
but we will arise and stand upright.

—Psalm 20:7-8

When I began to babysit for families in my neighborhood, I opened my own checking account. I recorded my earnings in a little blue book that I took to the bank with my mom or dad. I endorsed the check I'd received and handed it to the teller along with my bankbook. The teller would slide the book into a machine, adding the amount of the deposit to my book. A sense of security came over me when I saw the numbers increase. I never wanted to take money out of my account. I only wanted the numbers to increase. I could count on my money; I had earned it; it was all mine.

Years later, my husband and I put money aside to pay for our children to go to college. When the stock market crashed, our savings were diminished, and we worried about college tuition bills. We discussed financial aid with the college office and learned that they had lost too much money on their investments to offer any assistance. We had trusted in chariots and horses, as the psalm says—or cars and boats, bank accounts and investments.

Economic uncertainty brings us face to face with what we put our trust in. The more material wealth we have, the stronger the temptation to put our trust in it, as the psalm suggests. Financial security becomes a false buffer. Unlike counting on the market, placing our trust in God—finding our identity not in what we own but in whose we are—is true security that cannot ever be taken from us.

Trusting in God does not, except in illusory religion, mean that he will ensure that none of the things you are afraid of will ever happen to you. On the contrary, it means that whatever you fear is quite likely to happen, but that with God's help it will in the end turn out to be nothing to be afraid of.

—Jonathan Aitken
Former member of Parliament
of the United Kingdom

Second Sunday of Advent

Judah became God's sanctuary
and Israel his dominion.
The sea beheld it and fled;
Jordan turned and went back.
The mountains skipped like rams,
and the little hills like young sheep.

—Psalm 114:2-4

The second candle of the Advent wreath is lit today. Branches from the holly tree, sprigs of pine, and green ground cover with red berries are clipped and arranged around the candles. Our wreath with its four candles is built on the wagon wheel that finished the autumn harvest then fell off at the side of the field; turned on its side and brought in, it is adorned with greens and lit.

Take a piece of paper and write down the places where you sense the presence of God. Are there places in the natural world on your list, places by the ocean, on a mountain, camping under a night sky filled with stars? The tender green shoots of spring suggest the beauty of holiness. The sweet breezes of summer seem to come from heaven on a hot afternoon. In autumn, the green leaves of summer turn shades of yellow, orange, red, and brown before returning to the earth, filling the world with brilliant color. Winter's stark shapes point to the power of God.

In the inner city, sidewalks, pavement, and concrete dominate. But if you look carefully, in the summer you'll see rose bushes bursting with blooms climbing up the side of a house. My Vietnamese neighbors take the smallest piece of earth and grow herbs, cabbage, peppers, and onions. If you look out today on a city street, a country road, or the woods, even from your car window and even in winter, God's presence can be seen in the natural world.

Stop to give thanks today for the river you pass, the sunrise that begins your day, or the simple majesty of an old tree. Give thanks to God for giving us the cathedral of the natural world.

Lord, which is the more precious of these two blessings, that all things are means through which I can touch you, or that you yourself are so universal that I can experience you and lay hold on you in every creature?

—Pierre Teilhard de Chardin, SJ
Jesuit priest and paleontologist
(1881-1955)

Second Monday of Advent

Show me your ways, O LORD,
and teach me your paths.
Lead me in your truth and teach me,
for you are the God of my salvation;
in you have I trusted all the day long.

—Psalm 25:3-4

I sat down across from Sister Kay for our afternoon meeting. She looked at me with the no-nonsense expression I have come to rely on. I laid out what was troubling me, including my inability to understand how God was leading me. She listened, giving me all the time I needed to complain how impossible it was to know what to do, how frustrated I was with the inscrutability of God's will. When I finished, she said "God's horizon is not the same as yours. You are being asked to have faith and trust in what you cannot yet see."

We want understanding, and sometimes God removes it to grow our trust. That afternoon Sister Kay suggested that I pray with these words: "Show me what you want me to see." Then she said to leave the rest to God.

"Show me what you want me to see." This prayer frees up the whole enterprise. We give up the short view for the long view. Mary was given the faith to do this when the angel Gabriel came to her and told her to trust in what she could not see. Joseph, visited in a dream by God, was brave enough to surrender his plans and trust in what he could not see or understand.

Lord, show me what you want me to see.

By your Spirit, inspire our senses that
we may see as you do and hear as you speak.
And as we sleep, come into our dreams,
that our souls may awaken to you.

—Noël Julnes-Dehner
Episcopal priest and documentarian

Second Tuesday of Advent

For with you is the well of life,
and in your light we see light.

—Psalm 36:9

For people in the desert climate of Israel, a well was the source of water, and hence of life. Water was salvation. Wells saved lives. The well was the centerpiece of the village, the public gathering place.

A striking white alabaster statue depicting the story of Jesus and the woman he meets at the well sits in a window in the convent chapel of the Sisters of Saint Ann. Morning light beams into the space between these figures as their bodies lean toward each other in lively conversation, their hands extended, their bare feet nearly touching.

"This man knows everything I have ever done," the woman says, "and he doesn't condemn me. He knows about my five marriages. He knows I lost the man who truly loved me and was treated shamefully by the man I was then forced to marry. He sees me, not as unclean or impure, but from the inside out. He is not of my tribe or race and he is talking to me, a woman. I offered him water from the well, and he offered me water welling up to eternal life."

This living water quenches our thirst to be known and understood, from the inside out. Jesus comes to us and sits with us in the middle of the city, at a well at midday. He knows our stories and extends his hand to us, takes delight in us, and offers us water from the well of life that will never run dry. The woman sat on a stone at the side of the well that hot afternoon and in Jesus' light, she saw light. God's coming to us reawakens us to who we are.

Our vocation is not simply to be,
but to work together with God
in the creation of our own life,
our own identity, our own destiny.

—Thomas Merton, OCSO
Trappist monk, theologian, poet
(1915-1968)

Second Wednesday
of Advent

Those who seek after my life lay snares for me;
those who strive to hurt me speak of my ruin and plot
treachery all the day long.

—Psalm 38:12

Sometimes the enemy forces that seek to destroy us are not human beings. They are the principalities and powers of darkness: "Discipline yourselves, keep alert. Like a roaring lion your adversary the devil prowls around, looking for someone to devour. Resist him, steadfast in your faith" (1 Peter 5:8-9a).

The intelligent, cunning force of wickedness that rebels against God will continually attempt to sabotage our prayer life. Do you hear a critical voice when you approach your prayer? It may suggest to you that you will never get it right, that you don't have time to pray, or what you did yesterday should make you ashamed to pray. The voice might tell you, "The car is no place to pray to Almighty God. Find a more respectful place to pray than during your commute!" Or perhaps,

"God does not want to hear all your mixed-up words. Stop jabbering. This isn't real prayer." Or, "You can't pray while you are on a run or on your morning walk. Give God all your attention." Or, after you pray, "All you could give God was fifteen minutes—the monks pray five times a day."

The spirit of darkness lays snares for us, seeking to separate us from closeness to God, from praying in everything and at all times. If I had to guess what Satan's most despised verse of scripture is, I'd say it's "Pray without ceasing" (1 Thessalonians 5:17).

When we are not aware of its voice and potency, the power of darkness makes inroads and sets up roadblocks. When we are seeking God, as we are this Advent, the dark power perks up and goes to work. Be vigilant, pray for protection, but be not afraid. Jesus is profoundly acquainted with evil, and the demons flee from him. They cannot tolerate his light and steadfast mercy. Call upon his power. He is gracious and quick to come to our aid.

The Lord is faithful...[and] will strengthen you and guard you from the evil one.

—2 Thessalonians 3:3

Advent and Christmas Meditations

Second Thursday of Advent

Commit your way to the LORD
and put your trust in him,
and he will bring it to pass.
He will make your righteousness
as clear as the light
and your just dealing as the noonday.

—Psalm 37:5-6

No secrets are hid. Not from God. This is the good news and the bad news. The good news: when I am innocent, God knows. The bad news: when I am guilty, God knows.

I watched Sister Jeanette put these words into action. She was the chaplain at the women's prison and I was the assistant chaplain. As I came to know the incarcerated women, I heard their stories: crime scenes, arrests, vendettas, drug deals, courtrooms, sentences, plea bargains, parole violations, stories of innocence and guilt. With no judgment in her voice, Sister would look a woman dead in the eye and say, "The truth will set you free."

How much of what I do each day is done in secret, as if no one is watching? There are the lies, big and small, the taking that which is not mine (because no one will notice), the half-truths to protect myself, the façade to make things look okay when they are not.

Transparency. Nothing is hidden from God. When we eat in the dark or drink in the closet, lie about gambling, cheat on our spouse, or use money for a purpose not intended by those who gave it to us, we are seen by a God to whom "all hearts are open, all desires known, and…no secrets are hid." This prayer that begins Holy Eucharist reminds us that our lives are transparent to God. This is why forgiveness is central to our faith—we need to come clean. We can do it now. God is waiting and, if we ask, will give us the grace and mercy to amend our lives.

Cleanse the thoughts of our hearts by the inspiration of your Holy Spirit, that we may perfectly love you, and worthily magnify your holy Name; through Christ our Lord. Amen.

—The Holy Eucharist: Rite II,
The Book of Common Prayer

Advent and Christmas Meditations

Second Friday of Advent

*Be my strong rock, a castle to keep me safe,
for you are my crag and my stronghold;
for the sake of your Name,
lead me and guide me.*

—Psalm 31:3

New Hampshire, where we have our home, is called the Granite State. There are granite rocks hidden in the woods that are big enough for four people to sit on. When you dig in the earth to plant daylilies or asparagus, you dig up rocks of every size and must set them aside before planting. Rock walls border our meadow; rocks line the edge of our pond; rocks rest in the garden. "Be my strong rock," the psalmist tells God—doesn't ask, but tells, tells God to be "a castle to keep me safe."

I like to think of God as a rock. It is a metaphor that speaks of God as heavy, immovable, no soft edges to push in, no easy budging, no shifting under foot. The composition of rock causes it to stay cool when the temperature is warm and retain heat when the temperature grows cold. Rocks are the bedrock of life.

Be my strong rock, I pray today; be the solid, immovable force I can build my life upon. Be the beautiful smooth stone I carry in my pocket, the sailing flat skipper I throw into the sea. Let me live inside God, a castle of rock that will keep me safe, so solid that my bad moods, fleeting thoughts, and distracted mind might have a place to call home.

"Rock of ages, cleft for me, let me hide myself in thee" (*The Hymnal 1982*, #685).

My hope is built on nothing less
Than Jesus' blood and righteousness;
I dare not trust the sweetest frame,
But wholly lean on Jesus' name.
On Christ, the solid rock, I stand;
All other ground is sinking sand.

—Edward Mote
Baptist minister and hymn composer
(1797-1874)

Second Saturday of Advent

Then you hid your face,
and I was filled with fear.

—Psalm 30:8

God was never more present to Jesus than in the moment he felt abandoned on the cross. In that painful moment God's face was hid. Jesus did not feel it, but God was with him. Jesus was being held in the palm of God's hand, even as he felt he was alone, filled with pain and fear.

A man left the comfortable suburb where he lived and bought a home in a poor urban neighborhood. He could have lived anywhere, but he sought out a community that included young and old, poor and professional, gay and straight, black and white. Having no children of his own, he chaired the board of a neighborhood charter school and participated in neighborhood associations that built up the community and made it a safer place for everyone to live. He came to our church and helped raise money to build our playground, oversaw our finances, and cooked community meals. Disappointments at work began a downward spiral, and out of nowhere he found himself in despair. I knew it would pass, but the nature of depression is that we feel it will never pass. The man felt abandoned, forsaken, as if God had turned away from him.

God is present, even when we cannot feel it or see it or know it. God's action is simply deeper than our feelings. This is why we practice faith in community. When darkness befalls me, I need you to be hopeful for me. When I feel God's absence, I need you to carry my faith for me. When God is wrapped in darkness for us, others will sustain us.

Advent is a dark season. God in Jesus shows us that even when we are fearful and cannot feel God's presence, God is with us.

It is when things go wrong,
when the good things do not happen,
when our prayers seem to have been lost,
that God is most present.
We do not need the sheltering wings
when things go smoothly.
We are closest to God in the darkness,
stumbling along blindly.

—Madeleine L'Engle
Author, Newbery Medal winner
(1918-2007)

Third Sunday of Advent

O God, you are my God; eagerly I seek you;
my soul thirsts for you, my flesh faints for you,
as in a barren and dry land
where there is no water.

—Psalm 63:1

The words "O God, you are my God; eagerly I seek you" rise not from duty or obligation or because saying them will make us better persons, or even because praying them is the right thing to do. These impassioned words come from the psalmist's desire and longing. Desire is an urge, an ache of often unknown origin. We can make ourselves go to the gym, but we cannot command or banish desire.

For those who observe the traditions of the Advent Wreath, the pink candle is lit today to signal a day of resting from the labor of the mind, a lightening up, a giving in to the desire and longing for God.

So many times we go to God dutifully, eager to get our prayer done with, to cross it off our list and get on with our day. Sometimes we make prayer into a chore, like working out at the gym, requiring discipline. When we light the pink candle of refreshment, this day bears a message: Notice your longing for God. Refresh the heart of God by your eager desire. That longing begins in God's heart and has found its way to you. Receive it. Today is a day to light the pink candle and enjoy God.

O Israel, wait for the LORD,
for with the LORD there is mercy.
With him there is plenteous redemption
and he shall redeem Israel from their sins.

—Psalm 130:6-7

Third Monday of Advent

Even my best friend, whom I trusted,
who broke bread with me,
has lifted up his heel and turned against me.

—Psalm 41:9

Pink Christmas punch danced with frozen berries and ice in a cut glass bowl. Woven pine branches hung from the ceiling, filling the room with fragrance. The neighbors who hosted the party offered a simple supper and invited all their guests to bring cookies. On a large cloth-covered table, platters, boxes, and tins filled with beautiful and delicious Christmas confections were on display. Musicians, young and old, played along as we sang carols. My family and I looked forward to these gatherings.

But then our church membership began to grow and the parish embarked on a renovation of our physical plant to expand our worship space. This project raised a great deal of conflict in our parish. Some choristers were angry and left the choir to protest the proposed changes. My neighbor "lifted up his heel and turned against me" and no longer invited our family to his annual Christmas party.

It happens—a best friend, a husband or wife, a sister, brother, mother, or father turns against us. Those with whom we sat at table and broke bread, those we once trusted, turn their heel and walk away. And we have done it to others, turned on those we once loved and trusted. Betrayal hurts.

Jesus advises us to love our enemies and to pray for those who persecute us (Matthew 5:44). Leave revenge to God; leave judgment to God. Pray for those who turn on you. It is often the only positive, productive, and self-respecting thing to do. Place them in the hands of God.

Love your enemies and pray for those who persecute you…
For if you love those who love you,
what reward do you have?
Do not even the tax collectors do the same?
And if you greet only your brothers and sisters,
what more are you doing than others?

—Matthew 5:44, 46-47

Third Tuesday of Advent

*We have waited in silence
on your loving-kindness, O God,
in the midst of your temple.*

—Psalm 48:8

Silence is not always appealing. It can be frightening. I used to be afraid of silence, afraid of being alone. Keeping active felt better to me. Extreme busyness was a way of avoiding silence. I was avoiding the me I had to face when I was still, the me who needed to be brought into God's presence.

Our vestry, accustomed to debating budgets and making decisions, went on a day-long retreat. We sat in a beautiful chapel, and our leader told us we would begin with fifteen minutes of silence. Afterwards our leader asked us what the silence was like for us. Our treasurer, a man who worked for a financial investment firm, sat with tears rolling down his face. He was a quiet person and devoted to our church community, giving generously of his time and money. He had three children and his wife was the vice president of a bank. He was unable to speak for some time. Then he said, "I guess I needed that. I have never sat in silence. It was scary at first and I wanted to leave, but then I felt overwhelmed by love."

Silence is like cleaning a room that clutters easily. Silence lets the mind rest from its continual movement. It is no wonder silence is God's everlasting language. It is not easy, but it is worth committing ourselves to a period of silence each day. Silence sets us free from the games of control and evasion that take up so much of our talking and action.

There is nothing like being still. It is perhaps the purest, truest form of prayer.

O God of peace, who has taught us that in
returning and rest we shall be saved,
in quietness and in confidence shall be our strength:
By the might of your Spirit lift us, we pray,
to your presence, where we may be still
and know that you are God.

—A Prayer for Quiet Confidence,
The Book of Common Prayer, p. 832

Third Wednesday of Advent

Do not be envious when some become rich,
or when the grandeur of their house increases;
For they will carry nothing away at their death,
nor will their grandeur follow them.
Though they thought highly of themselves
while they lived,
and were praised for their success,
They shall join the company of their forebears,
who will never see the light again.

—Psalm 49:16-19

I don't consider myself rich. You may not consider yourself rich. We are the people this psalm is speaking to. There will always be someone with a nicer car, a bigger barn, better vacations, and a larger house. That is one of the tricks our possessions play on us. We get what we want and then we want more. We are not satisfied. The psalm reminds us that riches give us position and influence, a feeling of success, but not contentment. Ask someone who has more than you whether she feels she has enough. Ask whether her money has brought a sense of purpose to her life.

My husband is not a churchgoer; he struggles with the liturgy. But he is a person who knows contentment. He does not want to increase the size of his business so that he can earn more money; he would rather have more time than more money. He has enough and is content to grow his business slowly and carefully.

The season of Advent allows us to practice contentment. Someone you know will probably get a Christmas gift that you wish you had been given. When it happens, that person can become someone you envy. Or you could be reminded to thank God for what you have and find contentment, not in the gift you didn't receive or in one you received but didn't like, but within yourself.

We will carry nothing away at our death.

When we have a spirit of thanksgiving
we can hold all things lightly.
We receive; we do not grab. And when it is time to let go,
we do so freely. We are not owners, only stewards.

—Richard Foster
Theologian and writer

Third Thursday of Advent

*Whoever shows me the sacrifice
of thanksgiving honors me.*

—Psalm 50:24

Look for good. We honor God by choosing to be thankful, and it transforms our perspective. With practice we get better at it.

I once entertained a visitor for a week. I found it easy to focus on what I disliked about her: she was quick to take care of her own needs and slow to notice anyone else's. She talked loudly. She reached to fill her glass with the best wine and did not pour any for others. She never helped me make the salad or do the dishes. I eventually decided I could choose to look at those qualities and focus on how much she annoyed me, or I could look for good: she read interesting books and liked to talk about them. She was a good teacher and honored in her field. She adored her sons and was devoted to her husband. She was quick to say yes to a walk, a swim, or a trip to the movies. She never complained. She liked to have fun. She appreciated all kinds of food. It was up to me whether to look at the good or the bad.

"God is good—all the time" is a refrain I have learned from the people of my church. It is not a Sunday mantra; they repeat it on the telephone during the week and in casual conversation. Their gratitude to God does not depend upon things going their way, on having money or jobs or possessions to be grateful for. Gratitude comes first, independent of circumstances. Gratitude is a conviction, not a feeling. This mindset is something we choose. It produces in us the capacity to look for the good in ourselves, in each other, in every situation.

Be grateful.

What Jesus wants and the church needs
are people who see life as an abundant field,
who work with abounding hope.
What Jesus wants are people
who want to labor for the harvest,
knowing that the reaping is hard, hard work.

—Herbert Thompson Jr.
Eighth Bishop of the Episcopal Diocese of Southern Ohio
(1934-2006)

Third Friday of Advent

Create in me a clean heart, O God,
and renew a right spirit within me.
Cast me not away from your presence
and take not your holy Spirit from me.
Give me the joy of your saving help again
and sustain me with your bountiful Spirit.

—Psalm 51:11-13

"Each day is a God, every day is a God, and holiness holds forth in time," Annie Dillard writes in one of her early books. Each day begins anew. Most mornings we begin the day by going to the bathroom sink and splashing water on our face or by putting our head under the shower. These verses of Psalm 51 are also found in the morning devotion in "Daily Devotions for Individuals and Families" in *The Book of Common Prayer* (page 137). We begin the day cleansing the heart, emptying the heart, readying it to be filled by God in the day ahead.

Returning to this prayer each morning allows us to ask God to do for us what we cannot do for ourselves, to forgive what is behind us, let go of it, and be in the present. A clean heart is a ready heart, emptied of yesterday, ready for today.

Left to clean my own heart, I get bogged down reviewing what I regretted eating yesterday, why I lost my temper, all that I did not get done, what I said that I should not have said. "Create in me a clean heart, O God, and renew a right spirit within me" is a prayer that lets God do the cleaning and lets us receive a fresh start for today from the source of all fresh starts.

We don't have to figure out how to do it; we only have to be willing to let God create in us a clean heart. We will need it again tomorrow.

Stay in the present, with a heart that God has made clean, just for this day.

Almighty and eternal God, so draw our hearts to you,
so guide our minds, so fill our imaginations,
so control our wills, that we may be wholly yours.

—A Prayer of Self-Dedication,
The Book of Common Prayer, p. 832

Third Saturday of Advent

LORD, you have searched me out and known me;
you know my sitting down and my rising up;
you discern my thoughts from afar.
You trace my journeys and my resting-places
and are acquainted with all my ways.
Indeed, there is not a word on my lips,
but you, O LORD, know it altogether.

—Psalm 139:1-4

The yoga instructor was a master teacher, having practiced for more than twenty-five years. He asked us to hold poses for a long time, until we became acquainted with sensations that were uncomfortable in the body and mind. "Getting closer to God allows us to come closer to ourselves, and in getting closer to ourselves we become closer to God," he said. Yoga means union.

The words of this psalm speak of an entirely personal link between our lives and God. Imagine God knowing us this closely. God "knit me together in my mother's womb" and "created my inmost parts" (v. 12). "There is not a word on my lips" that God does not "know it altogether" (v. 3). I want to be known in this way, and it is frightening. The psalmist understands our fear and says that if we decide to run, to "take the wings of the morning and dwell in the uttermost parts of the sea, even there your hand will lead me and your right hand hold me fast" (v. 8-9).

The practice of yoga, like the practice of meditation and contemplation, increases our capacity to leave our distractions. We may fear the unknown, certain that if we come closer to ourselves we will discover that we are unlovable. Fear of the unknown lessens as we take in that God already knows us this intimately and we can't do anything about it except ignore it or accept it. This is who God is. And we are meant to know and love ourselves as we are known and loved by God. This Advent, we can acknowledge our fear and give in to the immensity of God's love for us.

Love, love, love, love.
The gospel in a word is love.
—Traditional song

Fourth Sunday of Advent

*Out of the mouths of infants and children
your majesty is praised above the heavens.*

—Psalm 8:2

Children slid from the pews and ran down the center aisle of the church in front of me as the congregation sang the hymn before the sermon. We walked to our large hall and sat on a big cream-colored rug. Pieces of colored paper and markers in baskets were passed around. I set the timer for one minute of silence. "We will be quiet and listen to what we need to pray for today."

Gathering the prayers recorded on colored paper and the drawings of those children not yet able to write, we formed a line to return to church during the passing of the peace. The weekly tussle over whose turn it was to bring the prayers forward to the altar ended with two children walking in with the adults presenting the bread and wine. The children handed the papers to the priest, who blessed the children's prayers and set them on the altar.

I never threw those prayers away. Each week I added them to a big bag I kept in my office. When I needed the company of children, I would take a colorful handful of papers from the bag and read their prayers: "God, I am sorry I broke the lava lamp in the youth room and lied about it. I didn't mean to." "I pray for Grandma in the hospital." "Help me stop fighting with my sister in the car." "I like trees. Will you make them in more colors?" "Let the Red Sox win today."

"Let the little children come to me," Jesus says. "To such as these belongs the kingdom of God" (Mark 10:14). No wonder Jesus wanted to be with children: they have no premeditated plans or tricky questions and are present to the moment, spontaneous, quick to believe. Their imaginations are full of magic and mischief; they are resilient against evil and magnets to happiness.

This is their season. Children light up with the sense of anticipation in Advent. If you do not have children of your own, connect with a child and spend time in the world of a child this Advent. Most of Jesus' teachings about how to be with God, how to pray, how to talk to God, how to praise God, and how to humble ourselves are captured in the faith of children.

Fourth Monday of Advent

Put your trust in him always, O people,
pour out your hearts before him,
for God is our refuge.

—Psalm 62:9

"Simple trust is the beginning of everything," Mother Teresa writes. To pour out my heart to a friend or to Jesus, I need to trust them. Sharing what is on my heart, without hesitation or judgment, requires trust.

We pour out our hearts when emotions drive us to speech. We refrain from forcing our feelings to be reasonable or articulate. Our sentences may not make sense. We might begin with one thing and end up on something else. That story might take us down a path we had not anticipated. I pour out my anger and end up in laughter. I pour out my anxiety and end up thankful. When was the last time you poured out your heart? Maybe you have never poured out your heart and cannot imagine doing such a thing in prayer.

Today's psalm invites us to pour out our hearts, to have an intimate and open relationship with Jesus. Opening the heart is a central theme in the practice of yoga. When we open the space in our bodies where our physical heart dwells, we change. We become increasingly willing to open our hearts throughout the day.

When you feel strongly about something today, instead of filing it away or hoping it will get lost in the day's busyness, take time to pray. Save it until later if you cannot stop at that moment, but open your heart to God. See if this grows your trust in God's care for you. Simple trust is the beginning of everything.

Someone was once anxious,
wavering between fear and hope.
He prostrated himself before the altar and said,
"If only I knew such-and-such, I would persevere!"
He presently heard from within him a divine answer:
"If you knew that, what would you do?
Do now what you would do then,
and you will be perfectly secure."

—Thomas à Kempis
Medieval priest and writer
(1380-1471)

Fourth Tuesday of Advent

You brought us into the snare;
you laid heavy burdens upon our backs.
You let enemies ride over our heads;
we went through fire and water;
but you brought us out
into a place of refreshment.

—Psalm 66:10-11

Suffering is part of human experience. We don't like it and we certainly don't have to seek it, but what do we do when it comes our way?

Winifred is from Guyana. She left her country in search of a new life for her three boys and herself. She entered the United States in difficult circumstances, encountering the "snare" of having to find work to support herself, a place to live, and a green card enabling her to build a life for her boys. She had what she called a "heavy burden" on her back of having to raise children in the inner city, take the late night bus to work at a hospital once her boys were in bed, and see them the next morning in the school cafeteria where she went when she got off the night shift for her second job. She has gone through fire and water, and she is the first to tell you that God has brought her out time and again to a place of refreshment.

Look at the suffering you have endured. What has it done to you? Inspired compassion? Turned you bitter? Allowed God to make of you a stronger, kinder soul? All things come to us from God. And when suffering comes, God will take it and make of it a crown of glory.

When you are ensnared, when a heavy burden is upon your back, when your enemies are riding on top of you and oppressing you, ask God to bring you out to a place of refreshment.

Come to me, all you that are weary
and carrying heaven burdens,
and I will give you rest.

—Matthew 11:28

Advent and Christmas Meditations

Fourth Wednesday of Advent

He makes the woman of a childless house
to be a joyful mother of children.

—Psalm 113:8

Reproduction is not the same as it was in the first century. Having children is no longer understood to be the sole purpose of a woman's life. Child-bearing years begin later and last further into midlife. Many couples experience infertility. For some it takes years to conceive and have children. Others, after having their first or second child, are no longer able to conceive. Some people are blessed by advances in medical technology that enable them to increase or share their fertility and have children. Some couples enjoy marriage without children; others decide to adopt. And some young girls become pregnant long before they are prepared to care for a child.

Infertility is a roadblock in life that feels personal. I have met with couples who ask, "If children are gifts from God, why is God punishing us with barrenness? Could God give us a baby if he wanted to?" They don't like coming to church, seeing families with babies and children, and they sometimes leave in anger.

When we are angry at God, most of us walk away. What would happen if we went to God, honestly, with our anger? What if we imagined God on our side and asked for help? Mary did not expect to be pregnant; Joseph was likely very angry when he found out. What if we opened our mind to possibilities we have never before considered? Could we make peace with not having more children, or try an advance in reproductive medicine? Maybe it is time to look at adoption. What if, in the midst of it all, we uttered the words "Thy will be done" and believed the words were for us, not against us?

In this divine dance we are all dancing, God may lead but it is entirely up to us whether we will follow…
The only thing that is absolutely sure in this scenario is that we have a partner who is with us and for us and who wants us to have life.

—Barbara Brown Taylor
Episcopal priest and writer

Fourth Thursday of Advent

You have fed them with the bread of tears;
you have given them bowls of tears to drink.

—Psalm 80:5

Tears are a gift. What if God had made us without them? We are meant neither to hold them back nor to make too much of them. They are simply the apparatus God has given us to express feelings that run deeper than words: tears of joy, tears of sorrow, tears of pain. Some of us cry easily and frequently, while others can hardly remember the last time they cried. Tears are evoked by sights we see, by beauty, by the emotions of others, by music, by pain, loss, and tragedy.

People cry in church. Looking out at a congregation, I often see people in tears.

Leila is a strong woman who never misses a Sunday except when she goes home to Trinidad. The holiday season is tough on her. She wants it to be over before it begins, and what gets her through is coming to church. She gets the holiday blues—"Why am I so sad when everyone else is so happy?" The sting of loss, missing those we love and see no longer, or the pain of a family divided or a heart broken is heightened in the weeks before Christmas. Advent offers the consolation of God's love and understanding to the blues of this season, inviting individuals into community, into the family of God which welcomes us and offers balm to what hurts.

God feeds us with the "bread of tears" and "bowls of tears to drink" as certainly as with a crusty loaf of warm bread on our dinner table and a bowl of soup when we are hungry. Don't force upon your tears the tyranny of understanding. Let them be. Let them come. They are making sense of your life in ways your mind cannot. Let them release the joy of a wedding, the pain of a divorce, the sadness of grief, the loss of a loved one. Tears are a gift from God.

History is lubricated by tears. Prayer,
maybe most prayer (two thirds of the psalms are laments),
is accompanied by tears. All these tears are gathered up
and absorbed in the tears of Jesus.

—Eugene H. Peterson
Presbyterian pastor and author

Fourth Friday of Advent

Praise him for his mighty acts;
praise him for his excellent greatness.
Praise him with the blast of the ram's-horn;
praise him with lyre and harp.
Praise him with timbrel and dance;
praise him with strings and pipe;
Praise him with resounding cymbals;
praise him with loud-clanging cymbals.
Let everything that has breath praise the LORD.

—Psalm 150:2-6

Children light up when someone praises them, and so do I. Don't you? We are motivated and encouraged by praise. Praise lifts us up. It moves us forward. And praise is what we offer God. "Let everything that has breath praise the LORD," the psalm instructs us.

Josie volunteers at the food pantry on Tuesday mornings. I went to the funeral of her close friend who went to pick up milk at the corner store on a Sunday afternoon and was the target of a bullet meant for someone else. A week later, I called to see how Josie was doing. "Blessed and highly favored, Reverend

Cathy," she said. Sick with grief, she was taking the week off from registering the poor who come for food, and yet, in all things, she was praising the Lord.

Praise God for the smell of coffee brewing. Praise God for the night that is past, sleepless or restful. Praise God for this new day. Praise God for the orange you peel and the child you feed. Praise God for the animal needing water. Praise God for the gift you still need to find and the presents you have to wrap. Praise God when there is not enough time. Praise God when the day is too long and seems it will never end. Praise God for legs to take a walk and a voice to sing a song. Praise God for your taste buds and your eyesight. Praise God for the tree outside your window. Praise God for the snow. Praise God for your children, regardless.

What were we made for? What am I to do with my life? Praise God. Praise and thank God for everything that is. Give praise when things go well and when they don't. Praise when there is death and when there is new life. Choose to live a life of praise.

Fourth Saturday of Advent

"Be still, then, and know that I am God!
I will be exalted among the nations,
I will be exalted in the earth."
The LORD of hosts is with us;
the God of Jacob is our stronghold.

—Psalm 46:11

Christmas Eve, the final day of Advent. Hurried wrapping and last minute errands around town. The line at the Irish bakery snaked out the door and into the parking lot. Across the street men stood behind the fish counter wearing Santa hats, breathlessly serving both the grumpy and the cheerful. One customer asked for a few jars of cocktail sauce and a handful of lemons as he wrote a check and walked out with quarts of chowder, shrimp, and oysters on ice to take to his sister's for Christmas Eve. Everyone in line knew he was the uncle who delivered on Christmas Eve.

A family filed into the front row for the children's service. Everyone was dressed up—the girls with hair ribbons, the boys and Dad in bow ties. As the service began, we rose to sing "Joy to the World," and as the mother stood, she removed her coat. Her apron was still tied around her waist, over her Christmas outfit. Our eyes met and we laughed out loud. Later, returning the candles we had held as we sang in the darkened church to the basket in the back, she told me of rushing to church one summer morning only to look down the pew to see that her son had no shoes on.

The birth of Jesus to human parents in a human story reassures us that it is in our humanity, in the flesh, that we meet God. The beam of light streams from the manger where all the promises of God begin, in the incarnation of God in human time and history. God and humanity meet in the labor pains, apron strings, and shoeless children who gather to put their hope in Jesus, the Lord of hosts, now with us; the God of Jacob, our stronghold.

When all is said and done, this is a silent night and a holy night—a night, finally, to be still and know that God is God. What has been done has been done, what has not been done has not been done. Let it be. Let the stillness of this night enfold you, all those dear to you, and all those who have no peace.

Christmas Day

Mercy and truth have met together;
righteousness and peace have kissed each other.
Truth shall spring up from the earth,
and righteousness shall look down from heaven.
The LORD will indeed grant prosperity,
and our land will yield its increase.
Righteousness shall go before him,
and peace shall be a pathway for his feet.

—Psalm 85:10-13

It is here, the day we have been waiting for. No matter what the days of Advent have been like for you, today is a new beginning. The birth that took place in Bethlehem is "reborn in us today," as the hymn promises. God comes to the center of our lives, born in our hearts.

I had two brothers and two sisters, and we ran early to our parents' bed, tugging at them, begging them to get up and come to the tree in the living room, where the cookies we had put out for Santa were gone and the glass of milk left empty, streaked on the sides. My father sat in a chair and opened his Bible to read the birth narrative from Luke's Gospel, forcing us to wait before we pulled our stockings off the hooks and dove under the tree to find our names on packages. The story that took place in Bethlehem has come down through the centuries into this time and place with twelve days to let loose and celebrate.

The church I serve, St. Mary's, is an inner-city Episcopal parish in Boston, once the parish home of clergyman Phillips Brooks who in 1865 wrote the carol "O Little Town of Bethlehem" (*The Hymnal 1982*, #78, 79). Today the once prestigious neighborhood of Victorian homes is one of the most diverse zip codes in America. Poor and professional, black and white, gay and straight, immigrant and resident neighbors gather and sing:

> *O little town of Bethlehem,*
> *how still we see thee lie!*
> *Above thy deep and dreamless sleep*
> *the silent stars go by;*
> *yet in thy dark streets shineth*
> *the everlasting Light;*
> *the hopes and fears of all the years*
> *are met in thee tonight.*

Whatever today holds for you, fulfilled expectations or disappointment, sadness or joy, the star above the manger leads us to a birth that changes us like a newborn child changes an entire household. Nothing is ever the same again. God comes on Christmas in the person of Jesus and he takes up the room we have prepared for him over the past four weeks. We welcome him in with the concluding words of Brooks's hymn:

> *We hear the Christmas angels*
> *the great glad tidings tell;*
> *O come to us, abide with us,*
> *our Lord Emmanuel!"*

Merry Christmas.

> *For God so loved the world*
> *that he gave his only Son,*
> *so that everyone who believes in him*
> *may not perish but*
> *may have eternal life.*

—John 3:16

December 26

Saint Stephen, Deacon and Martyr

Be my strong rock, a castle to keep me safe,
for you are my crag and my stronghold;
for the sake of your Name, lead me and guide me.

—Psalm 31:3

The twelve days of Christmas, this brief festive season in our church year, is often lost in the aftermath of Christmas celebrations and plans for New Year's. School vacation week can change everyone's regular routine. Family members stay on to visit, filling the household. Our days are often filled with activities, making it difficult to keep to our pattern of daily prayer. Changes in our routine are not times to stop praying; they are times to pray in new ways.

Rather than stepping away from prayer when we are out of our routines, these times can enrich our practice, giving us an opportunity to follow the command in scripture to "pray without ceasing."

Instead of coming away from a meal to pray, let your taste buds praise God in the food you enjoy. Imagine your body without taste buds. How dismal!

Eating would then solely satisfy hunger pangs, which is not how God designed our bodies. Eating is pleasurable. Taste buds are God's gift; they declare the glory, the magnificence of God's crea-tion. Praise God for the meal you share and those you share it with. Let tasting food be a prayer.

Instead of getting time away in quiet and closing your eyes to pray, open your eyes and pray in the midst of a walk. When your eyes behold the quiet, snow-laden pine trees or shimmering city Christmas lights, pray in thanksgiving. When we feast our eyes on people we love but do not see at other times of the year, our sight can become an opportunity for prayer.

The birth of Jesus, the child in whom divine life shines, opens every particle of our being, down to the smallest detail of our life, to God's presence. Don't waste time feeling badly that you cannot find quiet time away for prayer this week. Let go of the discipline of prayer you have grown accustomed to, just this week, and, as Psalm 34:8 says, be led and guided to pray with your taste and sight. Far from diverting us from prayer, vacation weeks, travel, and unexpected events invite us to come closer to the ultimate goal: to pray without ceasing.

December 27

Saint John, Apostle and Evangelist

...though the wicked grow like weeds,
and all the workers of iniquity flourish,
They flourish only to be destroyed for ever;
but you, O LORD, are exalted for evermore.
For lo, your enemies, O LORD,
lo, your enemies shall perish,
and all the workers of iniquity shall be scattered.

—Psalm 92:6b-8

Roxi and Ralik, Stacia and Kyle are high school students in our youth group. On Sunday afternoons they rehearse with the steel drum band, brightening our parish with their energy. I like to sit and talk with them over Sunday brunch, the meal we share following worship. I remember what high school was like. It was not an easy time for me, and I think it is harder on them, today, than it was on me. I know they face strong temptation to follow a crowd that would not be the best for them. I know they want to work hard and do well and go to college, yet it often seems, as this psalm puts it, that "the workers of iniquity flourish." It is difficult to stay the course, hard to hear yourself think and follow God when all the powerful voices around you are telling you how to be cool, what to do, how to win a place inside the group, and what will cast you outside it. Whom do you trust?

A wise bishop who raised four children of his own once told me to talk to God about my kids, more than I talk to my kids about God. Young people are pressed so hard they almost fall, as Psalm 118 says. The power of darkness that seeks to draw us away from God is a fierce current. And young people work hard to swim against it.

Young people need our prayers: our children, our nieces, nephews, grandchildren, neighborhood kids, our students, our patients. Bring to mind the young people you know. Thank God for them, be a rock in their life, give them strength. Believe in them. Be someone they can trust. Through you, the Lord will come to their help, and steer them right. Don't underestimate the importance of being in their life. They need our prayers and our attention. It is not easy for any of us to be true to God, and true to ourselves, but it is particularly difficult in high school. Pray for the young people in your life. They need to know that the "workers of iniquity" will not flourish. They need to know how the adults in their life have struggled to follow God, and that in the communion of saints, the church, we are here for them.

God our Father, you see your children growing up
in an unsteady and confusing world:
Show them that your ways give more life
than the ways of the world,
and that following you is better than
chasing after selfish goals.
Help them to take failure,
not as a measure of their worth,
but as a chance for a new start.
Give them strength to hold their faith in you,
and to keep alive their joy in your creation.

—A Prayer for Young Persons,
The Book of Common Prayer, p. 829

December 28

The Feast of the Holy Innocents

If the LORD had not been on our side,
when enemies rose up against us;
Then would they have swallowed us up alive
in their fierce anger toward us;
Then would the raging waters
have gone right over us.
Blessed be the LORD!
he has not given us over
to be a prey for their teeth.
We have escaped like a bird
from the snare of the fowler;
the snare is broken, and we have escaped.
Our help is in the Name of the LORD,
the maker of heaven and earth.

—Psalm 124:2-3, 5-8

Herod the Great was continually in fear of losing his throne. Appointed by the Romans in 40 BC, he governed Palestine for thirty-seven years. He was famous for his barbarity. Fearing the loss of his seat to an infant king born in Bethlehem, he ordered all male children two years of age or younger in Bethlehem and the surrounding regions to be slaughtered. Today is dedicated to these Holy Innocents, the children who died at Herod's hands whom Augustine called "buds, killed by the frost of persecution the moment they showed themselves."

Today's psalm consoles us with a remarkable promise. These innocent children, and all children whose lives are snatched from them by barbarity, matter; they count. God does not give us over as prey to the teeth of those who kill us. The heavens above and the earth beneath declare God's power and promise to bring his children to everlasting life. A sparrow does not fall from the tree and an innocent child's death does not go unnoticed.

Newborn Jesus, now just five days old, will grow up and die an innocent victim's death, like so many other human beings, united with them in a death like theirs. His rising is what makes his story history. His death, like that of any other innocent victim, joins him to the worst of human tragedy. But his rising sets him apart. Bigger than death he opens up the heavens above and the earth below and claims them for himself as witnesses to a life beyond what someone can do to end our life.

Every day I read in the paper or hear in the daily news of the death of an innocent victim. Today, let us pray for them. Pray that the snare of the fowler will be broken, that the designs of evil tyrants will be frustrated, and that God's rule of justice and peace will reign. Give glory to the Lord, the maker of heaven and earth, for the life of all innocent victims and for every soul received into the arms of God's mercy.

Do not let your hearts be troubled.
Believe in God.
Believe also in me.
In my Father's house
there are many dwelling places…
And if I go and prepare a place for you,
I will come again and will take you to myself,
so that where I am, there you may be also.

—John 14:1-3

December 29

My God, my rock in whom I put my trust,
my shield, the horn of my salvation,
and my refuge;
you are worthy of praise.

—Psalm 18:2

Roland stands a lanky six feet, three inches tall. A handsome black man, his hair graying at his temples, he walks to the food pantry from his home, four blocks up the hill. His first words as he approaches me in the kitchen are: "Where two or three are gathered together in his name, God is in the midst of them."

Members of my city parish often quote the scriptures. Knowing the Bible by memory allows them to bring the word into our conversations. "God's peace and his love to you, Reverend Cathy. How are you?" Winnie says when she sees me, sounding like Saint Paul. When you call her at home her voicemail greets you with these words: "May the face of God shine upon you and be gracious to you, and may God's peace and his love be with you today and forever, please leave a message after the beep." As Theresa comes into the church on Sunday morning her first words are not "hello" or "good morning," they are: "Behold, and see how good and pleasant it is when brothers and sisters dwell together in unity!" When I ask Veta how she is, she replies, "Blessed as usual, blessed and highly favored, Reverend Cathy."

Reciting verses from scripture as we go about our day gives us strength. It forms our perspective and keeps us mindful of God's presence.

Memorize a verse of scripture like the one from today's psalm, so you will have words on the tip of your tongue that have the power to turn your trust to God as you go about your day. The words we choose to greet one another, the words we say and repeat, carry power with them to shape how we live our day and how we influence the days of those around us. The scriptures become a living word traveling with us and creating an atmosphere that brings us back, throughout our day, to the presence of God. Words of scripture cast light across a face, or a room. They are "a lantern to my feet and a light upon my path," as Psalm 119 in the service of Noonday Prayer reminds us.

Saying the words of scripture as we go about whatever we do today reminds us we are not alone. We are being guided, and we can place our trust in that guidance.

For whatever was written in former days
was written for our instruction,
so that by steadfastness and by the encouragement
of the scriptures we might have hope.
May the God of steadfastness and encouragement
grant you to live in harmony with one another,
in accordance with Christ Jesus.

—Romans 15:4-5

December 30

The Lord is my shepherd; I shall not want.
He maketh me to lie down in green pastures;
He leadeth me beside the still waters.
He restoreth my soul;
he leadeth me in the paths of righteousness
for his Name's sake.
Yea, though I walk through
the valley of the shadow of death,
I will fear no evil;
For thou art with me;
thy rod and thy staff, they comfort me.
Thou preparest a table before me
in the presence of mine enemies;
thou anointest my head with oil;
my cup runneth over.
Surely goodness and mercy shall follow me
all the days of my life,
and I will dwell in the house of the LORD for ever.

—Psalm 23 (King James Version)

This is the psalm said in the cramped foxholes of war, under the fearful hum of MRI machines, in the patient waiting room of an oncology unit—the most memorized psalm, the most beloved, the psalm we say together on Sundays, or at funerals and burials—the psalm our grandmothers gave us, printed and framed, edged with pastoral scenes of gentle shepherds guiding their sheep. Mine hung on a nail next to my bed.

I never tire of its soothing familiarity, or its comforting message. Being led by God to lie down in green grass freshly mowed on a summer day; walking by glassy waters, and feeling the peace across the surface of stillness.

The consolation is most keenly felt as the psalm travels through the dark valley, the shadow of death, and promises that even there, God's hand leads us. Fear no evil, the psalmist says.

As this year draws to its close, take a walk into the Twenty-third Psalm. Rest in the meadow, gaze at the river, hike down into the valley of shadows—where boulders and darkness seem to prevail, and we are easily lost.

Tired, and hungry we come to a table abundantly spread with a feast, before our enemies, before all that seeks to draw us away from the love of God:

the people, the voices, the temptations, the demons. Triumphing over all that puts us down is what raises us up: the table of the Lord. Here is the nourishment, power, and strength; oil anoints us, a cup is running over with the promises of God, a feast is spread out for us.

No matter the heights we climb to, or depths we fall to, nothing will part us from the mercy and goodness of God that is with us now as we pray the Twenty-third Psalm.

Grant, O Lord, that as the years change,
we may find rest in your unchangeableness.
May we meet this new year bravely,
sure in the faith that while people come and go
and life changes around us,
you are ever the same,
guiding us with your wisdom and
protecting us with your love.

—William Temple
Priest and essayist
(1739-1796)

December 31

God is our refuge and strength,
a very present help in trouble.
Therefore we will not fear,
though the earth be moved,
and though the mountains be toppled
into the depths of the sea;
Though its waters rage and foam,
and though the mountains tremble at its tumult.
The LORD of hosts is with us;
the God of Jacob is our stronghold.

—Psalm 46:1-4

I missed his midnight call from the hospital. Listening to the message on my machine the next morning, I heard a voice broken with anguish and fear. Bobby's son was in his room with the door closed, and he didn't respond when his dad called him. Bobby knocked on his door; no answer. Wondering if he had his headphones on, Bobby walked in to find his twenty-one-year-old son having a stroke. He called the ambulance and Isaiah was rushed to the emergency room. Bobby sat next to his son's bed waiting for him to wake up, overcome with fear. Five years earlier his eldest son had been killed in a violent assault on his band during a rehearsal.

"I feel bad that I call upon God when I am in trouble and forget about him when things are going well. I should call upon God all the time," Bobby told me as we sat together in his hospital room. God doesn't mind, Bobby: God is a very present help in trouble.

When I was a child, my most fervent prayers were said in the back seat of our station wagon on the drive to the dentist. I knew God could not erase from my teeth decay caused by the candy I ate. I prayed because I was deathly afraid of sitting in the dentist chair, of the sound of the drill and the pain of dental work.

In times of trouble we are keenly aware of our need for help, for God, for people to pray for us and be with us. Don't hesitate to pray when you are in need or trouble. Don't worry that you forget to thank God for things when they are going well. How else do we learn? Go to God when you are in trouble. Then when the trouble subsides, let the experience of God's nearness and comfort increase your prayers in every circumstance.

January 1

The Feast of the Holy Name

As far as the east is from the west,
so far has he removed our sins from us.

—Psalm 103:12

The first day in a new year—a natural time for resolutions and new beginnings.

Imagine a map of the United States of America— as far as New York City is from San Francisco, so far has God removed our sins from us. Imagine driving a car or taking a train or bus across this country. Imagine the states you would pass through, the endless miles of highway, how many times you would stop to refill your gas tank. All that distance and more, from the east coast to the west coast and farther, so far has God removed our sins from us.

We cling to our sins, but God doesn't. God takes less interest in them than we do. God is always ready for us to begin again, to start over—not full of regrets, but as fresh as a canvas awaiting the brush.

Holding on to the past, thinking it could have been different than it was, is a strong temptation, and when

Advent and Christmas Meditations

we give into it, it binds us, keeping us from moving forward.

There are things I wish I had done differently as a young mother. If I had known then what I know now, I would have had more patience and confidence and been firmer about my convictions. I would not have been so busy. I would have paid closer attention. Accepting the mistakes I have made is humbling. Knowing how ready God is to forgive me, to release me from the past, makes all the difference.

Knowing that God forgives helps us make restitution where we can, and, when we can't, to envision the forgiveness of God separating us from our sin as far as the east is from the west. In that broad, open space is the freedom to begin again.

There is a wideness in God's mercy
like the wideness of the sea;
There's a kindness in his justice,
which is more than liberty.

—The Hymnal 1982, #469

January 2

The Lord is near to the brokenhearted
and will save those whose spirits are crushed.

—Psalm 34:18

I love to read Howard Thurman's poem "The Work of Christmas" at this time of year. It seems to be written for our spiritual reflection during the twelve days of Christmas. And it recognizes that the celebration of the birth of Jesus includes our actions on behalf of those who are suffering.

> *When the song of the angels is stilled,*
> *When the star in the sky is gone,*
> *When the kings and princes are home,*
> *When the shepherds are back with their flock,*
> *The work of Christmas begins:*
> *To find the lost,*
> *To heal the broken,*
> *To feed the hungry,*
> *To release the prisoner,*
> *To rebuild the nations,*
> *To bring peace among brothers,*
> *To make music in the heart.*

—Howard Thurman, "The Work of Christmas"

I remember feeling lost one Christmas when I was going through a divorce and returned home alone. Nothing seemed the same. I didn't know what to say to people or how to accept the loss I felt. And I did not know how to share it. This time of year is hard for many people. The season brings to mind those we have lost in death, or divorce, or tragic illness.

Thurman's poem tell us that the *work*—not just the celebration—of Christmas begins when the stillness comes back into our lives, after the friends have gone home and the relatives have been delivered to the airport. When the star in the sky is gone, we are not alone. It is time then for Christmas to truly begin. It begins with our actions, in the caring for others that accompanies our rejoicing in the Savior's birth.

It is a blessing, as Christians, that our faith teaches us that our actions are as important as our words. This time of year, when we gather for our celebrations, is also a time for compassion, a time to reach out and expand the table of God to include those in any kind of need or trouble.

January 3

He shall live as long as the sun and moon endure,
from one generation to another.
He shall come down like rain
upon the mown field,
like showers that water the earth.
In his time shall the righteous flourish;
there shall be abundance of peace
till the moon shall be no more.

—Psalm 72:5-7

One spring evening, as a day of rain came to an end, I went out to the porch. The showers that cleansed the earth and rocks lifted the fragrance of green grass and lilac blossoms into the air. I looked up and saw both ends of a rainbow. One touched down beyond the meadow and rose in stripes of color as high as I could see into the sky, and then came arching down and ended above the pine trees in the distance. A few moments later I went inside while my daughter remained outside. Then I heard her yell, "There are two!" Arching high across the evening sky were double rainbows.

God gives and gives and gives. This vivid demonstration of the majestic beauty in creation, the collision of rain and sun that produces a rainbow, reminded me that time doesn't belong to me, but to God. "In his time," the psalm says; in God's time, the rainbow said. As long as the sun and moon endure, God will be faithful, giving us what we need in due season, light when everything gets dark, friends when we are lonely, guidance when we are lost. Beyond what we even know how to ask for, God gives.

I take so much for granted: the opportunity to learn how to read and write, never going hungry, having more clothes to wear than I need, legs and arms and all five senses, a place to call home at day's end, friends and family to share life with. And that is just the beginning.

A thankful person is thankful in all circumstances. A complaining soul will complain even in paradise. We have the power to decide which one we will be.

Thank you, God, for everything;
for in everthing, you are there.
Amen.

January 4

The singers and the dancers will say,
"All my fresh springs are in you."

—Psalm 87:6

Mozart felt as if he was taking dictation from God when he composed music. A spark of the divine was in Michael Jackson's dancing from the time he was five years old. A singing voice, operatic as Pavarotti's, lyric as James Taylor's, or earthy as Willie Nelson's, has the power to transport us to another realm. The psalmist is drawing our attention to the source of artistic expression, so full of the fresh springs of creativity that give us a direct experience of divine life.

Christ is the life force of divine energy in you and me that we behold in singers and dancers. Jesus lived for thirty-three years, healed and taught, and disclosed the power of God. Even in January, when the parties are all over, and we are back to work, back to school, back to our routine, even then, the life force of Christ pulses within us.

"All my fresh springs are in you," the psalmist says. The kingdom of God is within us; not just in some of us, but within every single one of us, pulsing with fresh life, even when the season is dark, spring a long way off, and the holidays over. Christ is the originating spring, the center of our life from the waters of our baptism. The Holy Spirit connects us to the well that will not run dry, but will flow, overflow, all the way to eternal life.

*Those who drink of the water that I give them
will never be thirsty.
The water that I give will become in them
a spring of water gushing up to eternal life.*

—John 4:14

January 5

The LORD shall give strength to his people;
the LORD shall give his people the blessing of peace.

—Psalm 29:11

Being at peace. The blessing of peace is something God gives us, and it is always waiting for us.

It's hard to find peace when I think I must first resolve my problems, smooth out the conflicts in my relationships, get to the end of my list of things to do, as if peace is something I give myself. The truth is that peace is given to me.

The psalm says that peace is a blessing God gives to us. That blessing is not reserved for rarified moments of completing a demanding assignment or resolving a divorce or custody battle or lawsuit. Peace from God is always waiting for us, always something God wants to give us.

One day, I noticed I was at peace. It surprised me. I was not seeking it, or looking for it, and I was surrounded by many unknowns. I was leaving one job, without any certainty of what lay ahead. I was torn in several directions, unsure which path to take.

The peace that came to me was a peace that I had always wanted—to be free of anxiety, even for a brief moment; to be at peace not because my relationships were perfect, or I was satisfied with myself and my life. No. Peace that passes all understanding, the peace that God gives, can be something we pray for and then one day, without effort or warning, perhaps just when we need it the most, we stop and notice that we are at peace.

Step away today from the people at home and work. Close the door to your room, or go find a quiet church that is open, or a library, or the chapel in a hospital or airport. Be still. No ideas, no words. Whatever is troubling you, acknowledge it before God, and for the time you are praying, let it go. Relax your body by breathing deeply. Sit comfortably and rest in the cessation of words. Ask for the blessing of peace in the midst of all that is not right with your life. Notice that peace is there. You may not feel peaceful, but can you sense that beneath all the frenzy and unknowns the Lord will give you the blessing of peace.

The silence that God has placed at the center of our being will not fail us.

January 6

The Epiphany

Be joyful in the LORD, all you lands;
serve the LORD with gladness
and come before his presence with a song.

—Psalm 100:1

Epiphany is the name of a tuition-free Episcopal middle school for low-income students in my neighborhood. The school's headmaster is the most joyful person I have ever met. Each morning he wears his bow tie, dress shirt, and blazer and stands at the door at 7:00 a.m. when his students walk across the threshold for breakfast. Three meals are served to the students, and they complete their homework after dinner before going home. The motto of the school is "We never give up on a child." The teachers are demanding, uncompromising with discipline, and loving. The school exudes joy and the desire for excellence.

On Sunday mornings, when the headmaster could be resting in bed and taking time for himself, he gets up and comes to church to serve at our altar. He brings food to share at brunch even if he cannot stay to eat with us. He brings joy with him; he serves the Lord with gladness.

Parents of his students have threatened him. He has had his laptop stolen and money taken from his wallet. His teachers have been in crisis and his building projects took impossible turns. His life, like yours and mine, is not happy all the time. But he seems to have made a decision to be joyful—not to fake it, but to be it. It is as if he has set his feet in the stream of gladness, not the muddy pond of the troubling hassles that fill each day. He grows angry, disappointed, and discouraged, and people get mad at him. But the words of this psalm, "Be joyful," ring in his heart and twinkle in his eye.

Knowing this Christian headmaster has been an epiphany for me. God has made something clear to me through this man. I may wait forever to "feel" joyful because there is so much to feel sad or anxious or angry about. Choosing to *be* joyful, making gladness the atmosphere that surrounds us—the way we live in the world—can have a profound and lasting effect on the people around us.

Be joyful!

About the author

Cathy H. George serves as associate dean and director of formation for Berkeley Divinity School at Yale University. She draws inspiration from the teachings of Jesus and the natural world where she enjoys walking, swimming, gardening, and snowshoeing. She and her husband have two adult children.

About Forward Movement

Forward Movement is committed to inspiring disciples and empowering evangelists. While we produce great resources like this book, Forward Movement is not a publishing company. We are a ministry.

Our mission is to support you in your spiritual journey, to help you grow as a follower of Jesus Christ. Publishing books, daily reflections, studies for small groups, and online resources is an important way that we live out this ministry. More than a half million people read our daily devotions through *Forward Day by Day,* which is also available in Spanish (*Adelante Día a Día*) and Braille, online, as a podcast, and as an app for your smartphones or tablets. It is mailed to more than fifty countries, and we donate nearly 30,000 copies each quarter to prisons, hospitals, and nursing homes. We actively seek partners across the Church and look for ways to provide resources that inspire and challenge.

A ministry of The Episcopal Church for eighty years, Forward Movement is a nonprofit organization funded by sales of resources and gifts from generous donors. To learn more about Forward Movement and our resources, please visit us at www.forwardmovement.org (or www.adelanteenelcamino.org).

We are delighted to be doing this work and invite your prayers and support.